More Farm-Raised

DEVOTIONALS

Ida Mae Couch

ISBN 978-0-578-98010-2

Bible scripture NIV unless otherwise noted
Cover design: Ida Mae Couch
Cover artwork: Richard Lee Phillips
Photo credit: Manika Logue

Printed in the United States of America
Published by Lobry Publishing

You can reach Ida Mae at:
LobryPublishing@gmail.com

Or on Instagram
@ lobrypublishing

For my brother and sister
Mitchell Walton
and
Inez Cline

Contents

Beginnings

I grew up listening to Elvis music. My mom really liked Elvis. She had most of his albums.

Mom would tell a story about when she and my dad were just getting to know each other. It was the fall of 1955. I only state that because Elvis was just getting started in his music career. He was doing shows in small towns, and this was likely at the Lawrence County Fair. This is how the story went:

Elvis was coming to the area to perform, and my mom wanted to go. Dad, who resembled Elvis at the time, had tickets, but he had already invited another girl. My mom hoped he would change his mind, but he didn't. He took the other girl.

Little did Dad know he would live to regret that decision. How was he to know they would end up getting married, having three kids and how each one would hear about that bad decision he made; breaking our mom's heart like that?

The story was all told in fun. I don't think Mom held a grudge over this. It may have been a sore, but not a grudge. It made a great story to tell us, too, about how their relationship began.

Colossians 3:13 says, "Bear with each other and forgive whatever grievances you may have against each other. Forgive as the Lord forgave you."

Pinching Furniture

We had a couch and rocking chair that Mom
and Dad had purchased as a set. The frame
was wooden, and it had vinyl cushions. As
with anything that gets used over time, they
began to show their wear and the piping
around the cushions started to crack.
Whenever I would get up from sitting there,
the piping would "pinch" my leg, and, boy, did
it hurt! It would leave marks too. My brow
would furrow, and I would truly feel angry. It
had hurt me, and I wanted to hurt it back.

Unexpected hurts like that can be shocking
and bring anger to the surface really quickly.

In life, we experience unexpected hurts that
often bring out unpleasant reactions similar
to what I felt when those cushions pinched

my legs. Isn't that often our reaction to being hurt?

One of the fruits of the Spirit is self-control. As we mature, we hopefully become less easily triggered and are better able to retain our composure. It takes practice and forethought to grow to this point, but it has its rewards. People have greater respect for those who are cool-headed and can think before they speak.

"A fool gives full vent to his anger, but a wise man keeps himself under control,"

Proverbs 29:11

Wishy-Washy

My mom made most of my clothes when I was little. She'd take me to town, let me pick out fabrics that I liked, and then she would make me something.

I was around five years old, and I was outgrowing some of my church dresses. So, Mom took me to the store, and I picked out some fabrics. One of the fabrics was white with raised polka dots, and then it also had a heart design printed on it. I also picked out a pretty, pale yellow. I think I remember getting a soft pink gingham too.

Mom made me three dresses from what we bought and hung them in my closet.

Well, the dresses hung there and hung there, and Mom asked me why I wasn't wearing the new dresses she had made me. I told her I didn't like them. "But you picked out the fabrics," she would say. "I know, but I don't like them." So, they continued to hang in my closet.

The next year, when I was REALLY outgrowing my church dresses, and nothing was fitting at all, I took another look at those dresses Mom had made me. I put one on one Sunday morning and decided that it was a nice dress and I could wear it. The next Sunday I tried another, and it went from there. Mom asked me one day what changed. I told her I decided I liked them. It was as simple as that.

I honestly don't remember why I decided I liked them. Maybe it was desperation because I didn't have anything else to wear, but the point is, I came around and did make use of the dresses.

We can be fickle creatures, can't we? We vacillate from one side to the other.

Elijah had to deal with some people who couldn't decide who their god was; the Lord God, or Baal. In 1 Kings 18:21, he asks them, "How long will you waver between two different opinions? If the Lord is God, follow Him; but if Baal, then follow him."

God doesn't wish us to be fickle or wishy-washy. He desires us to be solid in Him.

"So then, just as you received Christ Jesus as Lord, continue to live in Him, rooted and built up in Him, strengthened in the faith as you were taught, and overflowing with thankfulness."   Colossians 2:6-7

Birthdays

We celebrated birthdays, but not in a big way. There was usually cake, a few gifts, and birthday spankings.

Birthday spankings were a big tradition in our house. However old you were turning was how many spankings you received from each family member, and then there was an extra "one to grow on."

I remember being turned upside down over my brother's shoulder and carried through the house as he announced it was spanking time. He would give me his share of licks. Then my sister would come and count hers off quickly. Mom would be behind her pattin' my behind next. There were lots of giggles going around.

My 6th birthday came just as Mom was finishing up nursing school. Grandma Carr had been taking care of me for the past several months, but my time with her was almost finished. I would begin school in the fall.

I have vivid memories of my gifts that year. I received a green school satchel with black trim, and it was filled with all kinds of school supplies. There was writing paper with large spaces and dashed lines that beginning writers used to help learn how to make letters. There were thick pencils and crayons because, at that time, they believed thicker meant better for young hands. I found a bottle of glue and a small pair of scissors tucked down inside the satchel as well. Being a picky eater, Mom knew I would be taking my lunch to school every day. So, a lunch box was also part of my birthday surprises. I was set to begin school.

Family traditions create bonds.

In the Old Testament, there were many traditions kept by the Israelites. One of those was the Passover where they remembered God releasing them from slavery. Every year they kept the memory alive through special meals and other activities.

Just as we carry memories from our family traditions, I'm sure kids grew up remembering events from their own family's celebrations. As we do, they probably shared those memories with their kids and grandkids.

Events and memories help us form bonds with "our people," whether it's with our relatives or our church family.

As part of God's family, congregations meet every Sunday to remember Jesus' sacrifice and cherish the hope and freedom we have in our faith. It forms a bond and that is part of God's plan.

Meeting Laura Lynn

I remember the day I met Laura Lynn for the very first time. She and I were the same age and would be starting school soon. Our moms had known each other for a long time and thought it would be nice for us to have familiar faces to recognize in our new environment.

I remember the car pulling into our driveway. Laura Lynn got out, and I remember she had long blonde hair in two ponytails and the biggest, blue eyes I'd ever seen. Our moms introduced us, and we became friends that day.

Laura Lynn and I would sometimes go home with each other after school. I remember going to her family's farm several times through the years. I loved going there because her farm was a little different from mine; they had animals. I remember cows and chickens…and cats. We both loved cats.

I also remember playing around the clothesline where her mom hung laundry to dry. We would play a type of hide-and-seek around the sheets.

Mom would pick me up after she got off work, and I was always so sad to have to leave. The time flew by when I was there. I would hope that my mom would stay and visit her mom for a bit so we could have a few more minutes to play.

The expression "time flies when you're having fun" is very true. Those visits were like a flash in the pan, and I couldn't believe how swiftly it passed.

This makes me think of this verse:

"Yet you do not know what your life will be like tomorrow. You are just a vapor that appears for a little while and then vanishes away." James 4:14 NASV

One of the concepts I take away from this scripture is we aren't in control of our time here, and we need to take one day at a time. God is the one in control, not us. We need to use the time we have well.

My Name

Is there anything more personal than our name?

Both of my grandmother's middle names were Mae...Elva Mae and Pearlie Mae. And I had a great aunt named Ida Mae. My dad liked how that sounded. So that's how I got my name.

Would you believe there was another "Ida" in my class? She came to our school, I think, in fourth grade so I was around nine years old. To distinguish the two of us, it was decided that she would be Ida (her name was Ida Margaret), and I would be Ida Mae. In the South, it isn't uncommon for girls to go by both their first name and middle name together...like my friend Laura Lynn. But that was the point at which I became "Ida Mae."

When we hear our name, something special rings inside us. There have been studies about how teachers can impact their students by calling them by name in a learning environment, that they respond and are stimulated in positive ways when they hear their name called.

Do you think about God calling your name? Scripture says he does.

Isaiah 43:1 says, "This is what the Lord says—he who created you, Jacob, he who formed you, Israel: 'Do not fear, for I have redeemed you; I have called you by name, you are mine." (ESV)

He also has written your name in the palms of His hands. (Isaiah 49:16)

Your name is also recorded in His book of life. (Philippians 4:3, Revelation 20:15)

Your name is called, claimed, written, recorded...

You have a God that loves you.

Wintertime Chills

Getting up and ready for school on cold winter days was a challenge. The source of heat for our home was only a floor furnace in the living room. To save money, Mom and Dad turned the thermostat way down at night, and we used blankets and quilts to keep warm as we slept.

I dreaded coming out from under my covers on those days because the air in the room was cold, the floors were cold, and the clothes I had picked out the night before to wear to school would be cold too. So, I came up with a system to avoid having to deal with the unpleasantness of coldness.

I began by wearing socks to bed so that when my feet touched the floor first thing, they wouldn't feel the cold wooden floors. I also laid my clothes at the foot of my bed. The heat from the electric blanket would keep them from feeling so icy in the morning. I even learned to get dressed without even leaving my bed! I was one clever girl!

Isn't it interesting how we adapt to situations to avoid uncomfortable things?

This makes me think of Jonah. He is the poster child for avoidance.

In the first chapter of Jonah, God told him to go to Nineveh, but Jonah didn't want to preach to the people there. We've likely all heard about how that ended.

But consider how far out of the way he went to avoid doing what God told him to do. What if he had simply gone and done what he was supposed to do? Well, we wouldn't have the story of him being swallowed up by the big fish... But look at the trouble he caused himself by running away from his task instead of simply doing it.

We can be quite clever when it comes to getting out of doing something we don't want to do. But what if instead of avoiding it, we just faced it and did it.

Are you avoiding anything?

A Bank's Grand Opening

Life stayed fairly constant in our little rural area of the world. Very few changes happened there. So, when there was a change, everyone knew about it and took notice.

I remember a new building being constructed in our small town that looked quite fascinating. The architectural style was modern and had a space-age feel. We learned it was to be a new bank, and when construction was completed, we attended the grand-opening celebration.

I remember walking in through the bronze-shaded, glass doors and being amazed at the size of the building. It was two stories tall, and we got to tour both levels. The interior was dressed with fancy carpeting, and modern designs painted on the walls in golds and browns. It had drive-through teller windows where capsules were sent through vacuum tubes. I had never seen anything like that before, and being a gadget lover, I was enthralled.

My parents established their banking there, and I remember going through the drive-through with Mom one day. I was mesmerized watching that capsule zip through those tubes with a push of a button into the bank where the teller dealt with the transaction. Then the capsule zipped back to my mom with the documentation of the transaction. (And the teller had put a lollipop in the capsule for me.)

I had a feeling of pride that our small town had arrived at a new age, and it stirred something inside me; it stirred amazement.

Things like this make me wonder how people reacted when they saw Jesus doing His miracles. Life was so primitive, and to see someone healed, or to even be that person, must have been indescribable. It would have been difficult to comprehend. Think about it for a moment. Go there in your mind. Imagine being in a crowd where this man, Jesus, is simply touching people, and they are being made well!

THAT is only a small portion of the power of God. I don't think it's possible to truly understand or comprehend all the power God has. He has allowed us to know about it, though. If we can keep our child-like perspective instead of trying to grasp it with our own logic, then we can still be constantly amazed by the things He's doing around us every day.

What will open your eyes wide today?

Big Scary Hill

Where I grew up in northeastern Arkansas, the land was very flat, which made it great for farming.

Not far from us to the east was an area of hills called Crowley's Ridge. My grandparents on my mom's side lived there.

To the west was the base of the Ozark Mountains. One of my aunts had moved to that area. Her family bought a log house near Imboden, and I remember going to visit them for the first time in their new home.

It was a Saturday adventure. I was sitting in my usual spot in the middle of the front seat between Mom and Dad. (The front seat of our car was all one big seat. There was no console in the middle. And we didn't wear seatbelts back then either.) Crossing Black

River took us from the flat country to the hill country. The roads became hilly and curvy. We made a turn to the south in Imboden and followed the paved roads a bit further. Roads in the backcountry weren't marked very well, but Mom and Dad had the directions my aunt had given them. They found the gravel road that my aunt had described, and this is where the adventure really began.

The road was red clay with chunky rocks of the same color. It was bumpy and noisy as we made our way slowly along the path. The road was just wide enough for two cars to pass.

We met a couple of other cars on the way, and the dust was as thick as fog. There were areas where the road was tree-lined, and the red dust had collected on the leaves. There were some particularly bumpy areas where rainwater had drained, and it rattled the car quite a bit. Mom and Dad called those areas "washboards" because it felt like you were driving across one with all the little peaks and valleys the drainage had caused.

We came to an area where there were several rolling hills in a row, and you couldn't see past the farthest one. I remember Dad driving up that final hill, and it seemed like we were going to be going out into space because you couldn't see the road continuing. It was like we were driving off a cliff! I panicked and grabbed my mom because I thought we were about to die. We crested the hill, and I was waiting for the car to leave the ground, but amazingly the road did continue on the other side, albeit quite steeply. That hill felt like it came back and met itself. It was so steep! I was happily relieved to see that we weren't going to die, but I was ready to get to my aunt's house. I wasn't enjoying this adventure anymore.

As we travel down our own paths of life, we are sometimes faced with parts of the road where we feel like we're going to go off a cliff, don't we? We wonder if we are going to make it to solid ground on the other side of a particularly difficult patch. These times can truly test how much we trust God.

In Hebrews 13:5-6, a promise is given:

"'Never will I leave you or forsake you.' So we say with confidence, 'The Lord is my helper; I will not be afraid. What can man do to me?'"

May you find strength and encouragement from these promises today or any time you are feeling overwhelmed with challenges.

Label Maker

Back in the '70s, a new product came out that allowed you to make your own labels using a hand-held tool. It was simply called a "label maker."

My sister had one of these cool tools, and I loved it. I remember there were many different colors of tape; red, black, blue, and green. I can remember making up reasons to make a label because it was fun to make them. I can also remember making a label with my name on it and I stuck it on my forehead. It seemed like a logical place to put it.

The purpose of a label is to mark where something belongs or tell what's inside a container. Or it could name who made the product.

I think of perfume bottles with fancy decorated labels. I think of canned goods with pictures of vegetables on their labels. We have labels inside our clothing to say who designed it, the fabric content and how to wash the item.

As people, we don't typically wear a label to tell what's inside of us, but what if we did? Some people like to put "labels" on people as a sort of pecking order. This went on in Jesus' day too.

I think of Matthew and Zacchaeus, who were both tax collectors. They were considered "less than" because of the role they played in society. They were the sinners that people avoided because of the "label" that had been placed on them.

If you had a label, what would yours say? Do you think of yourself as a container?

"Filled with love."?

"Full of hope."?

"Washed in the blood of Christ."?

"Filled with the Spirit."?

One we can all wear is "Made by God." He's the ultimate creator.

What does your label say?

Hand-Me-Downs

I've always loved clothes. I don't know what it is about us girls, but many of us do enjoy clothing and fashion.

When I was growing up, we didn't have a lot of money to spend on clothing. Mom made a lot of the clothes my sister and I wore, but every now and then, we'd get a bag of hand-me-downs from friends who had outgrown them. It was like getting a load of treasure when Mom would bring these home to us.

I remember there was this one dress that was too big for me, but too small for my sister. It was a tame orange color with a white inset on the front that had embroidery on it. It also had black velvet trim on the cuffs and around the white inset piece.

I couldn't wait to grow into this dress because it seems so modern and different. Mom saved it for me to wear when I got a little bigger.

I remember getting a bag full of goodies from my cousin. I thought she dressed so cool, and I usually wore those clothes to rags. I remember I wore one of those shirts in my school pictures.

I got a bag later in my teens from my future sister-in-law. She was/is short like me, but she liked to wear long skirts, and I loved what she gave me. I felt sophisticated, mostly because I admired her so much.

Hand-me-downs may have been looked down upon by some people, but not to us. It was new and different, and we never knew what we'd find. Yes, hand-me-downs were special.

Bible stories are like hand-me-downs. They get passed down from the older ones to the younger ones. Some of the stories we may not understand when we're younger, but we "grow" into them as we mature. Sometimes, the teachers that taught us these stories were very dear friends or family members, and we treasure the sweet memories of hearing it from them. It's all a sweet, cyclic part of life.

The next time you go through your closet, think about who might appreciate your hand-me-downs, whether they be material or spiritual. You may touch someone's heart in a special way.

Hand-Me-Downs
Part 2

I just shared a story about hand-me-downs and about how there was a particular orange dress that I really liked, and I couldn't wait to grow into it. Well, the dress was put in the closet away from sight, and we forgot about it.

One day mom was going through the closet and found it again. It had been a couple of years, and, sadly, I had grown too big for it. I was so disappointed. Fashion may have moved on from that "look," but I didn't care. I was still hoping to wear it when I grew into it.

This was an extremely minor disappointment in my life, and it may not warrant this comparison of disappointment I'm about to share, but it was a disappointment nonetheless.

How do we handle disappointment?

Paul, writing the Christians in Philippi, said that he had learned to be content in any situation.

Philippians 4:11-13 says, "...I have learned to be content whatever the circumstances. I know what it is to be in need, and I know what it is to have plenty. I have learned the secret of being content in any situation, whether well fed or hungry, whether living in plenty or in want."

But here's the meat in verse 13: "I can do all this through Him who gives me strength."

Yes, life will have disappointments, some major and some minor. We may feel unsettled or dissatisfied. We may experience times where we feel we're living in limbo. We may wonder what in the world is God trying to show us or tell us. Life isn't always going to turn out the way we plan or want it to, but in Christ, we can learn to be content.

New Tennis Shoes

All sorts of impossibilities are possible in the mind of a child. And something as simple as a new pair of tennis shoes can take a child's mind to imagine glorious feats...

Around our house, shoes were limited. You had your Sunday shoes, going-to-school shoes, and play-in-the-yard shoes. The play-in-the-yard shoes were last year's school shoes.

Robert's Shoe Store was on Main St., and it was filled with the smell of new leather. The store owner would measure one of my feet on a metal foot measuring tool to determine the size I needed. Then it was a matter of seeing what he had in stock. Mom was a practical shopper. The shoes needed to be a color that would go with anything. So, white it was.

I remember how it felt to put my feet into those new shoes and tie the bow tight. There was a fancy, tingling feeling that started in my toes, and it worked its way up and out the top of my head. Instantly these shoes made me walk better, take stairs better, jump and hop better. I was a new creature! I couldn't wait to get home and see how much faster they would make me run!

It was tradition to wear the new shoes home from the store, and oh! How my feet itched to be out of the car and let loose! The speed in these shoes was building by the minute. As soon as we were home, and Mom stopped the car, I jumped out and dashed up and down the driveway. That was just the warm-up to make sure I could handle the power. Once the warm-up was complete, it was time to become the Olympic champion I was to become in these new, fast, power-filled shoes.

My brother enjoyed track in high school, and I had seen him run many races. The familiar phrases "On your mark! Get set! GO!" were part of my childhood fantasy of this moment.

I began on one side of the yard and sped to the other in a blur. Oh, I was definitely faster...MUCH faster in these new shoes, and

Mom confirmed it. She had never seen me go so fast!

I would need to be careful with these new shoes. They held a great deal of power and energy...at least in my imagination.

Children can have wild imaginations. These imaginations can be quite inspiring. I believe all inspiration comes from God. God gave us the ability to be imaginative and the ability to dream of things beyond reality. Sometimes innovative ideas can be revealed through imaginations.

Paul speaks about the secret wisdom of God, and how He reveals what He wants to reveal in His time. Paul quoted Isaiah about unimaginable things.

"No eye has seen, no ear has heard, no mind has conceived what God has prepared for those who love Him." 1 Corinthians 2: 9

This was a prophesy of Christ and the salvation He would bring. No one could have imagined this. Paul speaks to this as something that has been revealed through the Spirit, and how what was once hidden is now shown. What a blessing to know this wisdom...

Other New Shoes

Out of the box, new shoes were stiff and tight. They would need to be broken in so that they weren't so uncomfortable. In the process of breaking them in, the backs of my heels would become raw where the shoes rubbed, even if I had the buffer of socks.

Mom usually carried Band-Aids in her purse as a remedy to cover the irritated, tender skin, but when she didn't have her purse stocked, it was difficult to walk! I remember trying my best to walk in a way that the shoes wouldn't keep rubbing that raw area.

We all go through times when we may feel a bit tender and raw like the tender skin where new shoes have rubbed. It's difficult to keep taking steps in our faith-walk when we're hurting, and we may just want to stop walking altogether. It may seem there is no buffer to protect us from the pain we're feeling.

This is what the Lord said to Joshua just after Moses had died:

"Be strong and courageous. Do not be terrified; do not be discouraged, for the Lord your God will be with you wherever you go." Joshua 1:9

I think it's safe to assume that Joshua was feeling raw and overwhelmed. Not only was he mourning the loss of Moses, but now he would be stepping into his new role as the leader of the Israelites. They were about to settle in the promised land, and the weight of it all certainly had to be heavy.

The Lord offered comfort to Joshua during this time of transition and pain by saying, "God will be with you wherever you go." This same promise is ours to claim today.

Be strong.

Be courageous.

Do not be afraid.

Do not be discouraged.

Because God is with you wherever you go...

even when your blistered heels are raw.

Thief in the Night

On the farm, it was necessary to have a fuel tank for the tractors and such. Ours was a large, gray, metal tank. It had a red nozzle like gas station pumps had in town, and I thought that was kind of cool. The tank sat in the back yard near the farm equipment.

Somehow Mom and Dad figured out that someone had been coming and filling up their car with gas during the night. There were no street lights out in the country, and we didn't have a dog to alert us if someone was sneaking around. Dad decided he needed to put a lock on the nozzle so that people couldn't come and freely fill their cars up anymore.

How frustrating it must have been to my parents to have someone stealing like that! If you've ever had something stolen from you, you know how violating it can feel.

Hopefully, every Christian knows that it is wrong to steal. After all, it is one of the ten commandments which are the very basics of who we are to be as God's children. What we may not realize, though, is that stealing can have different forms. We sometimes make light of pushing the "gray" boundaries between the black and white areas of right and wrong. Just like telling a "white" lie is still lying, we sometimes "take" things that don't belong to us.

Part of being godly, holy people is keeping our integrity in place. Something may seem minor in our eyes, but the intention and attitude of the heart aren't hidden from God.

"Or do you not know that wrongdoers will not inherit the kingdom of God? Do not be deceived: thieves...will not inherit the kingdom of God."   1 Corinthians 6:9-10

Mid-South Fair

Our family didn't take big vacations. We simply didn't have the money to do that. But we did have a few events that we anticipated and looked forward to each year, and one of those was the Mid-South Fair held in Memphis, Tennessee.

We would get up early on a Saturday morning and head east. It was about a two-hour drive from our house, so it seemed like a big adventure to my very young self. Mom would pack snacks for the car ride, and we would load up and hit the road.

One of the most anticipated parts of the trip was crossing the Mississippi River. "We're almost to the river," my dad would say, and we would get ready to look and see what all we could see. My young eyes, big as quarters, would peer out of the car windows absorbing this wide river and massive bridge. This also meant we were almost to our destination!

The Mid-South Fair had rides, food, carnival games, and craft booths where people sold their wares.

But one of the biggest attractions was the rodeo. I have LOTS of memories of that; horse parades, barrel racing, clowns, and of course watching the bull riders! Talk about intense! I remember those "cowboys" being around the edges of the arena, and if that bull started coming in their direction, they jumped up and over the fencing to get out of its way. And watching those riders hang on while those HUGE bulls tried to buck them off...why would anyone want to do that? If the rider fell off, those clowns would move in to distract the bull so the rider could get to safety.

Bull riding has an interesting point system. There are two sets of points. One set is for the rider. At a minimum, he has to ride for 8 seconds, and he isn't allowed to touch anything with his free hand. So, his score is based on his ride. The other set of points is based on the bull's performance; how agile he is...in other words, how hard or easy he makes it for the rider. If a rider isn't happy with his score, he may give up his first score, wait until everyone has ridden, and then he can have a second chance. There is a big risk with this option. If he gets bucked off on his second ride, he gets no score at all. A second chance for a bull rider must be carefully considered. It can be an all-or-nothing decision.

As believers in God and Jesus Christ, we've all been given a second chance. We have the opportunity to be forgiven and renewed. Are there risks in the decision to commit ourselves to this path? For many, yes. Family and friends may shun them. Some governments punish them...harshly. But is it worth it? Absolutely...

"He saved us, not because of righteous things we had done, but because of His mercy. He saved us through the washing of rebirth and renewal by the Holy Spirit, whom He poured out on us generously through Jesus Christ our Savior, so that, having been justified by His grace, we might become heirs having the hope of eternal life." Titus 3:5-7

The beauty of our second chance is that it is ongoing. We will still mess up, but the forgiveness and renewal are always available.

That is a win-win situation.

Callouses

When spring arrived, my favorite place to be was on my swing set. You could find me there climbing, hanging, and doing acrobatic tricks from the time I got home from school until it got dark. I only stopped for supper.

In those first few days of warm-weather playing, I would develop blisters on my hands. I would be forced to sit out a few days and let my hands heal because the blistered skin would come loose, exposing raw, tender flesh. I can still feel how tender they were. Just having air blow across these raw spots would hurt terribly. Mom would try to bandage them up so that my play wouldn't be interrupted, but that didn't help much because the bandages would come loose and not stay in place. I had to wait for my skin to grow back and become tougher.

In scripture, there is mention of callouses, but they aren't on people's hands. They are on people's hearts.

In Matthew, Jesus is quoting a prophecy from Isaiah and explaining why He speaks in parables.

"For this people's heart has become calloused; they hardly hear with their ears, and they have closed their eyes. Otherwise, they might see with their eyes and hear with their ears, understand with their hearts and turn, and I would heal them." Matthew 13:15

Jesus, the healer of hearts...

If these people could only have understood, with tender hearts, He would have taken care of the rest. But it was easier for them to hang on to their own ideas and understandings.

In order to accept the healing, it is necessary for the tender, raw spots to be exposed. And on this side of accepting the healing, we don't want the callouses to grow back. We need to keep our hearts tender and soft. We want Jesus to be able to tell us the same thing He says to His disciples in verse 16:

"But blessed are your eyes because they see, and your ears because they hear."

Badminton

Where did the name for that game come from? I'm sure there's some kind of story regarding that, and it probably came from England. I just remember watching and eventually playing it, from a very young age.

Mom kept the set-up neatly contained in the original box, and she would pull it out of storage in the spring. We had a net that we set up just off the front porch, four rackets, and several birdies.

Since we played very close to the house, the "birdies" would often end up on the roof. When we ran out of extras, we would have to try to retrieve them or wait for the wind to blow them down.

I also remember the rackets would develop "holes" in the mesh, and the birdies would go right through instead of being sent back across the net. This caused some playful jabs as points were missed.

All this talk of roofs and holes makes me think of an event in Mark 2 where some friends had heard about a man named Jesus who was able to heal people. There were a LOT of people who had heard of Him, and a large crowd had gathered. These friends couldn't even get to the door because the crowd was so thick. They had brought a friend of theirs who was paralyzed and hoped they could have Jesus heal him. I imagine they were pretty discouraged to see the crowd so large, but they didn't let that stop them. They were quite innovative and even daring because they went to the roof, dug a hole through the roof, and lowered their paralyzed friend down through the hole on a mat to get him to Jesus so He could heal him.

I'm not sure what is more amazing about this recorded event; the fact that Jesus healed him, or the fact that he had such determined friends! That is love being shown right there; deep love.

One of the things I take away from this is the faith of these friends. They believed that Jesus could heal their friend. What level of faith did they have to have to take the steps

they took? It was faith *without any doubt.*
That's why they were so determined. They
KNEW Jesus could fix the problem.

The next time you find yourself struggling
with doubt in your faith, I hope you'll
remember this story and find the
determination these friends had to keep
moving forward.

Siege

Those tiny, buzzing, pesky, biting, bloodsucking, flying creatures, also known as mosquitos, were the enemy. They surrounded our house and kept us locked in our home all summer. You took your life into your own hands if you exited the house because you were instantly attacked the second you opened the door.

That sounds like an exaggeration, but I kid you not. They were relentless and always, ALWAYS swarming.

I've often wondered why God created mosquitoes. They bite, leave itchy whelps, and just bug the daylights out of us. They're just such horrible little pests! And they robbed me of a lot of outside playtimes!

The worst was when one would make its way into our bedroom, and as we were trying to fall asleep, we would hear it buzzing right at our ear. No one rested until they were all smacked. So annoying!

While mosquitos aren't really an actual enemy, we have been given instruction in scripture about how we deal with our enemies.

Luke 6:27 says, "But to you who are listening I say: Love your enemies, do good to those that hate you, bless those who curse you, pray for those who mistreat you."

That list of instructions goes against our human nature. When we're being bombarded with personal attacks or someone just wants to make our life miserable, we tend to want to retaliate and even the score.

But Jesus, even as He hung on the cross, prayed for those who were murdering Him...because, as He said, they didn't know what they were doing (Luke 23:34). Jesus could see what was more important. He saw those people as souls...precious souls.

I know I need to do a better job viewing people that way. It's hard to look beyond our own personal feelings in times where we are being mistreated. It's a process, but God can and will help us change our perspectives if we allow Him to work in us.

Love your enemies.

Do good to those that hate you.

Bless those who curse you.

Pray for those who mistreat you.

They have souls just like you.

Blackouts

Every now and then, a storm would blow in, and knock out the electricity on our small farm. When this happened at night, there would be that initial shock of darkness when the power would go out accompanied by an eerie silence. We would sit for a moment to determine if the outage was just a blip or if it would be off a while. The only light available would be an occasional flicker of lightning from the storm. If the lights didn't come back on after a few seconds, Mom would feel her way to the kitchen to find a candle.

Mom would bring light back to the room with a strike of a match and touch the flame to the wick. The flame was timid and small at first. As it gained energy and strength, it would begin to stretch tall and eventually settle down into a steady burn. Our faces would glow in its light.

We would play with the flame by gently blowing on it, causing it to bend and distort a little. We would blow a little harder, causing it to sputter and waver. It would cling to the wick fighting to stay alive. If we blew too hard, the flame would die, and we would again be in darkness.

Darkness seems to carry an unsettled feeling. In the spiritual realm, darkness represents evil.

Scripture tells us that "God is light and in Him is no darkness at all." 1 John 1:5

There is nothing impure about God. This should bring us comfort knowing that our God is perfect in every way.

Jesus came and showed us how to be a beacon on His behalf.

"I am the light of the world. Whoever follows me will never walk in darkness, but will have the light of life." John 8:12

I encourage you to take this message to heart and trust that even when evil is trying to blow out your light, stand strong and cling to the life-giving source...Jesus.

From
Two Nurses
to One

After completing nursing school, my mom got
a job at the family clinic in town. One of her
good friends from church also worked there,
and they both worked for the same doctor.
Mom was so thrilled to be there and was
thankful she had her friend to lean on to
learn the ropes. They worked together for
many years and made a good team.

But sometimes financial adjustments have
to be made, and businesses have to make
tough choices.

The doctors had decided they couldn't afford
to each have two nurses, and needed to
narrow down their personal staff to just one

nurse each. They had a meeting with their nurses to inform them this would be happening, and based on performance, the decision would be made about who would be staying.

I remember my mom feeling conflicted and troubled. We went to church with this friend. She was a widow and needed that job to take care of her kids. But Mom needed this job, too.

I can't imagine how the doctors must have felt having to make this choice either. This was a gut-wrenching situation.

During difficult circumstances such as this, it may be hard to see God in the mix. All the emotions that surround an event like this can be overwhelming and blinding. Fear, uncertainty, anxiety...all these can shut our eyes to God's possibilities.

"The Lord is good, a refuge in times of trouble. He cares for those who trust in Him." Nahum 1:7

Feeling discouraged may also consume us, but what does the Bible say about feeling discouraged?

"In this world, you will have trouble. But take heart! I have overcome the world."

John 16:33

The choice was made, and my mom was able to stay on at the clinic. Her friend was able to find another job very quickly, and we were thankful for that.

It probably took some time for the wounds to heal, but the friendship remained intact. These two Christian friends weren't going to let something like this tear them apart.

"May the Lord of peace Himself give you peace at all times and in every way."

2 Thessalonians 3:16

Canning Corn

Every year Mom would order 100 ears of corn from a farm in Jonesboro to can for the winter. Dad would go pick it up and bring it home. Over the next few days, we would be shucking and cleaning the corn to get it ready for canning.

I liked shucking corn because sometimes when you pulled the husks and silks away, there would be a worm living in there. It was kind of gross, but that's what made it fun.

Once the husks and silks were removed, and all the tips were chopped off, each ear got washed in the sink. We stacked them in the drainboard and on towels on the counter.

Next, it was time to cut the kernels off the cob. I remember watching Mom cut down every side of that cob, and then she would scrape the cob a little to get more of the juice out. The corn was then transferred to a big yellow pan on the stove where it would be cooked and readied for the freezer.

Most of the corn was cut off the cob to be cooked and canned, but a few choice ears were set aside to be enjoyed over the next few days.

We cooked some right away so that we could enjoy some of our labor. The fresh corn would come out of the boiling water onto our plates. The corn changed in color from pale yellow to bright yellow. We would smother it with butter and sprinkle it with salt while trying not to burn our fingers. I remember biting into that first ear with eyes closed and taking in all the yumminess of it.

Then it was back to canning. We still had corn to get into containers and freeze.

Work is work. Sometimes work is really hard. It can become monotonous and sometimes consuming. But be reminded that even God took a rest and enjoyed what He had created.

In Ecclesiastes, it says, "...it is good and proper for a man to eat and drink, and to find satisfaction in his toilsome labor under the sun during the few days of life God has given him—for this is his lot." Ecclesiastes 5:18

Yes, there are tasks that need to be accomplished and hard work to do, but remember to enjoy the life you've been given even in the middle of it all. Take a moment to step out of the hectic pace and just realize where you are.

Find a way to pause and be grateful.

A grateful heart is a peaceful heart.

Deaf Dalmatian

Did you know that dalmatians have a 30% chance of being born with hearing difficulties? Well, it's true. And 5% of them are completely deaf. I had one of that 5% when I was a young girl.

The doctor my mom worked for bred dalmatians, and one of their pups was born completely deaf. Of course, they couldn't sell him. So, Doc asked my mom if we'd like to have him.

We didn't have many dogs when I was growing up, but we had a few, and Dalmie was one of them.

Dalmie was goofy, but I loved him. Since he couldn't hear, it was a little hard to control him. He and I would run all over the yard when I got home from school. I'd open the door to his pin, and he'd start jumping all over me, nearly knocking me down. We'd take off and run and run and run.

We didn't have Dalmie very long. Mom and Dad were afraid he'd run out to the road and get hit. Since he couldn't hear, it was a real possibility. So, we found a better, safer home for him. I would get reports every now and then about how he was doing.

Scripture tells of times when Jesus would heal deaf people. Mark 7 tells of a man who was deaf and couldn't speak. In verses 33-35, we see the description of Jesus opening his ears and loosening his tongue.

Then, Jesus tells them not to speak of this, which made them want to tell it all the more! Honestly, if you had seen that happen, would you be able to keep it to yourself? So, the news about Jesus' ability to heal spread quickly.

I'm sure it was an amazing time when Jesus walked the earth. The Bible tells us that He did so much more than what scripture tells us.

I truly cannot imagine...

Christmas Family Gathering

Every year around Christmas, my mom's side of the family would have a gathering. This was one of my favorite things because I looked forward to seeing everyone, and...the presents.

The gathering was held at my grandma's house, and I remember the excitement that came with getting ready.

Mom would be getting her part of the food together and wrapping it up so it would stay warm. We would help load all the goodies into the trunk of the car, and once the car was loaded, we were off to Grandma's house.

Soon, aunts, uncles, and cousins would begin to arrive, and Grandma's house would be overflowing with hugs, laughter, and happiness.

With the help of her daughters, Grandma would make a feast. There were some peculiar smells with all the holiday food. Most of it didn't appeal to me, but I wasn't there for the food. Some may have looked forward to Grandma's cooking, but I just wanted to get to the business of the presents.

I'd peruse around the table to see how close the adults were to finishing their meals. I would impatiently go whisper in my mom's ear, "When will y'all be finished? I want to open presents." Her typical response was, "In a little bit. Go play."

It seemed to take forever for everyone to finish their dinner. They just sat there and sat there talking and talking... And then they had to clear the table.

Then they had to clean up dishes.

Then they had to gather all the kids.

I'd be ready to explode by the time things were "ready."

Finally, we'd get to the part I'd been waiting for. Everyone would be called together, and Grandma's living room would be packed wall to wall with all of us sitting around. Adults got the couch and chairs, and the kids sat on the floor. We were pretty squished in there, but that was part of the fun.

One by one, different aunts would hand out gifts. There were lots of kids and little money, so there was some creativity in gift-giving. We typically got a mesh stocking filled with all sorts of Christmas candies and some other little trinkets.

But I remember one year one of my aunts was really clever. She made sleep shirts for all of the girls. She had taken fabric panels with bears on them that would typically be used to make into pillows, but instead, she sewed them onto large men's t-shirts.

The panel had a front and back view of the bear. She put the front of the bear on the front of the shirt and the back of the bear on the back. They were so cute. I wore mine until it fell apart.

My aunt was quite thoughtful putting those sleep shirts together for us. She got the reward of seeing our faces light up when we opened them. Her labor had been intentional, and she wanted to bring a bit of happiness and joy to her nieces.

"Remember this: Whoever sows sparingly will also reap sparingly, and whoever sows generously will also reap generously. Each man should give what he has decided in his heart to give, not reluctantly or under compulsion, for God loves a cheerful giver."

2 Corinthians 9:6-7

Whether we're giving back to God or giving to others, the attitude of heart is what really matters.

Lost Christmas Gifts

Christmas morning... You know that feeling. The presents are there waiting to be opened, and you can't open them fast enough to see what's inside. And as you're opening them, the wrapping paper just piles up around you. When all the presents are open, you scoop up all that paper and throw it away. Yes, that's how it was at our house anyway.

One year, after all the mayhem, Mom asked me if I liked my Shaun Cassidy t-shirt. I didn't get a Shaun Cassidy t-shirt. "What Shaun Cassidy t-shirt?" I asked.

Mom: "The one you got for Christmas. Didn't you open it?"

Me: "No, I didn't open a present with a t-shirt in it."

Mom to my sister: "Didn't you open a gift with earrings?"

My sister: "No, I didn't get earrings."

Mom: "Oh no! Where are they!?"

We looked under the tree, behind the tree, and around the furniture. Mom went searching in all her hiding places. She looked in her closet. She looked in her drawers and under her drawers. She looked in the bathroom closet and anywhere she could think of, but those gifts were not there.

We mentally replayed the morning chaos, and the only conclusion we could come to was that those gifts got gathered up with the trash and had been taken to be burned.

Oh, Man! A Shaun Cassidy t-shirt! I was so sad! I would have really liked that.

Do you remember the parable about the woman who lost one of her coins? In Luke 15:8-10, Jesus tells a story about a woman who has lost one coin. It says:

"A woman has ten silver coins and loses one. Does she not light a lamp, sweep the house and search carefully until she finds it? And when she has found it, she calls her friends and neighbors together, saying, 'Rejoice with me; I have found my lost coin.' In the same way, I tell you, there is rejoicing in the presence of the angels of God over one sinner who repents."

This is a wonderful representation to remind us how precious even one soul is to God. It's a happy day to learn someone who was "lost" finds Jesus.

Sitting on the Counter

When Mom would come home from work, she would immediately start dinner. I would sit on the kitchen counter and talk and talk and talk about my day at school. She would listen patiently as she peeled the potatoes or fried the ham. It was what we did.

It had never been an issue for me to sit on the counter until one day...

I was jumping down off the counter, and my pant leg caught on the cabinet door handle. I fell to the floor wondering what just happened. I had jumped down off that counter dozens of times without any problem. This time I caused some damage. It put a little rip in my jeans, but I had also caused the door hinges to bend, and the door didn't hang right or close properly.

My dad was a bit annoyed with me. He made it a rule not sit on the counter anymore.

Well, as with most habits, it was hard to stop hopping onto the counter and visit with Mom as I had always done. Dad was quick to remind me, and I would climb down carefully to sit on the floor or sit at the table, but it just wasn't the same.

Hebrews 12:11 says, "No discipline seems pleasant at the time, but painful. Later on, however, it produces a harvest of righteousness and peace for those who have been trained by it."

Eventually, I was allowed to sit on the counter again. Dad let the rule slide mercifully. I had learned to be more careful when I jumped down.

I felt terrible for causing that door to be permanently messed up. Dad was able to sort of fix the cabinet door, but it never closed the right way after that incident.

Burning the Trash

Out on the farm, we didn't have trash
services to take our trash away. We simply
disposed of it by burning it ourselves.

Groceries were bagged in paper bags back
then. Mom saved the bags and used them as
trash can liners. When the bag got full, it
was taken out to the burning barrel, which
was an old oil barrel. We took a little box of
matches with us to set it on fire, and it would
burn down to ashes.

This was my brother's job as long as he was
home. Then it was my sister's job sometimes
when he went off to college. Then it became
my job when she went to college. (Mom did it
quite a bit, and you're about to hear why.)

I had a hard time getting the trash to start
burning. Matches made me nervous. I

struggled with getting the match to catch fire. Once it was lit, I'd throw it in the trash bag as quickly as I could because they would burn down to my fingers too quickly. The match sometimes didn't stay lit when I dropped it like that, and I'd have to do it again. And if it was a windy day that added a whole new dimension to getting the fire started.

I would often go through several matches before I got the trash lit no matter the circumstances. It was frustrating and nerve-racking.

I had a healthy respect for fire. I knew the damage it could do if it got out of hand. Fire to me was equal to danger. It truly rattled me to think of the responsibility that went with it.

God is described as a consuming fire. In Deuteronomy 4:24, Moses is about to send the Israelites into their promised land, and He's warning them that they'd better not turn from God because He will scatter them and push them out of this beautiful land He was giving them. A consuming fire represented the power God had, and He deserved the awe and reverence of the people.

The same is true today. God is powerful, and He is deserving of our awe and reverence. Nothing should be more important than Him.

My Sister's Wedding

My sister was the first one of us kids to get married. I was around 11 or 12 when this all came about, and I was excited that something so big was happening in our family. I mean, a wedding is a big deal! (Wedding cake was my main interest, to be honest.)

As with most weddings, there were lots of preparations and plans to be made; choosing colors, invitations, flowers, bridesmaids and their dresses...and the cake.

Every little girl dreams of her wedding day. She has visions of herself in her beautiful dress, walking down the aisle to meet her groom. My sister was no different and looked at wedding dresses in pattern books and magazines to find just the right one for her. She made her own dress using white satin and lace. It was a beautiful, one-of-a-kind dress stitched with love and hope for her future.

A wedding represents the deep love, care, and affection shared between a groom and his bride. The love between bride and groom is very sweet, and even comforting because you have hope that this person is going to stand beside you through anything and everything and cheer you on.

As precious and special as our bride or groom is, there is another relationship that is even more precious.

In Isaiah 62:5, we are given this little jewel to help us understand the perfect love God has for us:

"As a bridegroom rejoices over his bride, so will your God rejoice over you." (ESV)

Yes, God rejoices over you. He cheers you on and celebrates you because He created you and loves you deeper than deep.

To What Length...

To what lengths will you go to be part of the crowd, to fit in? Apparently, some of us will do some pretty silly things. Well, I did anyway.

I remember sitting in Mrs. Weir's sixth-grade classroom. She was one of the best teachers ever. I learned so much in her class that year...in spite of my antics.

One of the popular boys sat in the aisle next to me, and several of his friends were in the same vicinity. They started playing this "game" of thumping each other's hands when Mrs. Weir would turn her back to write on the chalkboard. It was a contest to see how much pain they could inflict as well as tolerate. It was also to challenge their ability to keep it from Mrs. Weir's attention.

So, it went like this:

They would take turns sticking their hands out between the aisles when Mrs. Weir wasn't looking and thump the back of each other's hand as hard as they could. The pain would cause silent gasps, and there would be grimacing faces from the pain. As soon as Mrs. Weir turned around, though, all was normal...until she returned to her chalkboard. Then the thumping would resume.

Well, it looked like fun to me. So, one day I accepted the challenge by sticking my hand into the fray. Let me tell ya, it hurt. But I soon learned I was quite skilled at thumping. I was being challenged by the guys to see if they could handle my high-level of pain-inducing whops. It was gratifying to see that I could thump with the best of them.

I did not, however, want to attract Mrs. Weir's attention for these shenanigans.

"But for those who are self-seeking and who reject the truth and follow evil, there will be wrath and anger." Romans 2:8

I can assure you, there would have been some wrath and anger if we had been caught by Mrs. Weir. I would also have had to face my parents. The sad thing is I was willing to take the risk.

This is not good or healthy behavior.

It's easy to allow ourselves to be misguided even when we know we're not doing the right thing.

"Yet at the same time, many even among the leaders believed in Him. But because of the Pharisees, they would not confess their faith for fear they would be put out of the synagogue; for they loved praise from men more than praise from God." John 12:42-43

Be watchful of where you put your worth. It's better to please God than to please man.

My Brother's Student Teaching

When I was in the 6th grade, my brother was getting ready to graduate from college. He was studying to be a teacher. When it came time for him to do his student teaching or practice teaching, he had a unique opportunity to come back to our school and learn under one of his former teachers, Mr. Green.

Mr. Green was a wonderful, laid-back teacher. He taught social studies and geography to middle schoolers. (And he was Laura Lynn's uncle, so that also made him special to me.) It just so happened that Mr. Green's classroom was right next door to Mrs. Kellum's classroom, which was my classroom.

I hadn't seen much of Mitch in recent years since he had been away at college, but now we rode together to and from school every day. I saw him many times throughout the day walking down the hall and going in and out of the classroom next door. I was proud he was my brother, and I liked bragging about him to my classmates. I felt important because my big brother was there being an authoritative adult. I liked being associated with him because I thought it gave me a boost in how others saw me. It was a pride thing.

When Jesus was here doing His ministry, His apostles were likely proud to be a part of His "circle" like I was proud to be associated with Mitch. They were just outside the spotlight at times as crowd control and helpers. Maybe they saw this as advantageous and that they were a bit special because they were a "close friend" of Jesus. After all, Jesus, in their eyes, was going to re-establish the "kingdom" and they saw themselves as being a major part of that "kingdom." They viewed Jesus as the ultimate authority figure, and they were His right-hand men. They even asked Him who was the most important among them. (Luke 22:24). Jesus made it clear that it was not about position in society. In fact, He told them the first would be last, and the last would be first.

With Mitch being at school, I had thought it made the light shine a little brighter on me. Typical, I would say, of an 11-year-old. But the lesson isn't about the light shining on us. We don't shine brighter because of who we know or what circle of friends we belong to. It shouldn't even be about us being in the spotlight. It's about being a vessel and letting God's light shine out from us.

The light should shine *from* us, not *on* us.

Summer Camp

Oh, how I loved summer camp! I loved all the new activities there were to do like swimming and softball. I loved learning new crafts. One year we made a rocking chair out of clothespins, and I painted mine yellow.

I loved making new friends, too, but some of the people that came were from my hometown.

One year, a girl I sort of knew was there. I didn't know her well, but I learned some things about her that week that were hurtful.

We had been on lunch break and had some free time. I went back to the cabin to get something, and I found my sleeping bag and some of my belongings on the floor of our cabin. I didn't understand what had happened and didn't understand why someone would do that. I was terribly upset.

So, we found our cabin counselor and showed her what had happened. I don't remember all the details, or how we even found out who did it. I just remember being hurt, and feeling betrayed because we learned it was the girl from my hometown who had done it.

My opinion of her changed quite a bit after that. When I would see her at other church events, I would steer clear of her. She represented "trouble" to me, and I wanted to avoid that as much as possible.

It's sad that there are people like that in the world, but people who do things like this are people that are hurting. I didn't understand that at the time, and even if I had, I'm not sure I would have felt any differently. Being mean is simply unacceptable.

So, how do we deal with hurtful people? I'm not sure I have the answers even in my mature years. I do know that Jesus told us to love our enemies and pray for those who want to hurt us or persecute us (Matt 5:44). It doesn't say we have to interact with those people and some people are not "healthy" to be around.

Stepping back and looking at things from a broader view can give some perspective. It's easy to get caught up in the emotions of a moment when we've been wronged. Our feelings may come raging out, and grudges formed. But if we look at life in the "big picture" and see this person as someone who is in need of grace, we might be able to see them as a soul instead of an enemy.

And it doesn't hurt to remember we have all been given the opportunity to be covered in grace ourselves.

So, pray for those that want to hurt you or cause you harm in some way. You never know how God may work in that situation.

96

Blood-Related

Since my brother and sister were older than me, there came a time when I was the only one left in the house. There were no brothers and sisters around for companionship. When we went on little excursions, I was allowed to bring a friend along. Since we didn't do this often, it was a special treat.

On one of these day trips, we went to Memphis to visit the zoo and Graceland, Elvis' home. Mom was a huge Elvis fan, and when they opened his house for tours, she wanted to see it.

I was allowed to bring a friend and Stephanie was who I asked to go with us.

We went to the zoo first. I don't think I had ever been to a zoo before. I didn't quite know what to expect. I loved monkeys as a kid, and that exhibit was the one I enjoyed the most.

In the gift shop, I found a toy monkey. It was a stuffed toy attached to a stick with elastic string. When you slung the monkey out, it bounced back. Hours of fun, right? Stephanie and I each got one because we were having fun slinging them at each other in the gift shop.

We went on to Graceland, and it was a bit of a disappointment for my mom because the actual house wasn't open; only the grounds around his house were able to be toured. So, we didn't stay there long.

It was time to head home, and Stephanie and I sat in the back seat with our toy monkeys flying through the air at each other. Occasionally the monkeys would get tangled up together and get stuck in midair. We thought it was hilarious and would do this over and over with wild, preteen laughter that filled the car.

My dad wasn't used to driving in Memphis, and he needed to concentrate on the roads and not make a wrong turn. Our back-seat laughter wasn't helping him, and he told us to tone it down. For some strange reason, that made it that much harder to stop laughing. (Why is it that when you need to be quiet, things that are not-so-funny seem to be the funniest?) Stephanie and I kept playing quietly, in the back seat with our monkeys. We would get so cracked up, but we had to keep it silent. Oh, the belly aches we had from laughing so hard without being able to let out the laughs.

Sadly, the elastic strings on our monkeys broke before we got home, but we had certainly made some memories playing with them.

Stephanie and I considered ourselves as sisters and still do. We've known each other since we were babies. As close friends, we shared so many experiences and memories together...as true sisters would.

John 1:12-13 says, "To all who received Him, to those who believed in His name, He gave the right to become children of God—children born not of natural descent...but born of God."

God wanted us to have a sense of family among his followers. In the Old Testament, there were tribes and that kept that family feeling in place. But once Jesus came, and

99

the salvation doors were opened to all, God wanted to continue that sense of "family" among all His people. The language used in the New Testament calls us all brothers and sisters. This was part of God's plan to help us stick together.

Stephanie and I will never be blood-related as the world views relatives, but we **are** blood-related in Christ.

Fence Line

As with many farms, there was a fence line along one side of our property to mark the boundaries. Over the years, trees had grown along it, and the wire fence was barely visible. This line of trees had been there for as long as I could remember.

At some point, my dad's health began declining, and farming became almost impossible for him. We had a neighbor who helped us keep our land farmed, and he suggested we plow down the trees because it would make it easier for him to farm our land next to his, more continuous. It made sense.

But I was pretty attached to those trees, and to see them come down was a bit sad for me.

One Sunday afternoon, my friend, Stephanie, came over to visit, and we walked across the blank field to the tree piles. It was a mess of tree trunks, limbs and old wire. We climbed the precariously laid trunks to get to the top where we sat and contemplated life.

Even though the visible boundary was gone, there was still a boundary there.

God is a god of boundaries.

Many would rather ignore the boundaries and do as they please, but just because you don't "see" them or acknowledge them doesn't mean they aren't there.

The best-known set of boundaries is probably the Ten Commandments found in Exodus 20:3-17.

God gave these to be clear on what He expected of His people. When we break down these "boundaries" we can see that God put these in place as a type of protection. He didn't put them in place as punishments but as guides.

There is nothing new under the sun, and even though He gave these commandments, people still moved away from them and did what they wanted to do, just as many do today.

Isn't it interesting that many of our laws today are still based around these ideas?

Don't murder. Don't steal. Don't give false testimony against someone else. Adultery is still grounds for divorce in our system.

Other matters have to do with the heart in regards to how you treat your parents, how you desire what others have, or how you honor and worship God.

We see people today rebelling against these "boundaries," and for those of us that "know" God's requests and try to honor them, it's hard to watch people cross them with such disregard.

It's about free will. It's about choices. And it's about the heart...

"The heart is deceitful above all things and beyond cure. Who can understand it? 'I the Lord search the heart and examine the mind, to reward each person according to their conduct, according to what their deeds deserve.'" Jeremiah 17:9-10

Stay focused and mind the boundaries.

Learning to Drive

I've heard different tales about people's
experiences with learning to drive. Some
were eager to get behind the wheel and gain
that independence while others were a bit
more timid, and scared of it. I was one of the
latter.

I remember one random day as we made our
way home from town Mom asked, "You want
to drive the rest of the way home?" I said,
"Sure." She pulled the car off to the shoulder
of the road and we switched seats. I put the
car in "drive" and off we went. I was really
nervous, as any first driver is. I respected the
power of the vehicle and dared not move too
quickly because I truly didn't know how to
maneuver this boat, I mean car. (It was a
Plymouth Gran Fury from the '70's.)

There was an intimidating curve on our road that had to be navigated right off the bat. I crept quite slowly around it without any problem, but as soon as the path went straight, I ran off the road a couple of times. I remember hearing the gravel slinging around. I was ready for this ride to be over, but I still had about a mile to go.

There was a small bridge to cross, and I hoped I didn't hit the railing, or worse, miss it and fall into the ditch below it. I guess I made it because I don't remember anything traumatic happening.

Turning into the driveway was the next challenge, and then I had to manage to pull the car into the carport without hitting the support post or running into the house. I was relieved when I was able to put the car in "park."

Days later when we were once again returning home from a trip to town, Mom asked if I wanted to practice driving again. "No," was my reply as I looked out my window to the fields going by. A few days later I was asked again. "No, that's okay." Mom would tell me I needed to learn, but I was content being a passenger.

Sometimes in life we choose to be the passenger. We let someone else lead and take responsibility for how we will get from point A to point B. We trust they will get us where we need to go, and we don't think about it for ourselves. We just coast along.

Spiritually speaking, this can be dangerous. We take in what others tell us, but we don't check the information out ourselves. We blindly trust that what we are told is "gospel."

"For the time will come when people will not put up with sound doctrine. Instead, to suit their own desires, they will gather around them a great number of teachers to say what their itching ears want to hear. They will turn their ears away from the truth and turn aside to myths." 2 Timothy 4:3-4

On the highway of life, be the driver to your spiritual destination.

Driver's Ed

In the summer between 9th and 10th grade, my parents enrolled me in Driver's Ed. They saw that my reluctance to drive was not going away, so maybe working with someone else would help me take the next step. It was also a way for me to spend some time with my friends, and that was always appealing.

Mr. Warnick was our teacher. Talk about a man of patience... I never saw the man get ruffled. Well, maybe twice. But he was so calm with us as we learned how to give the car gas and then use the brake. You know the staccato of those first tries...start, abrupt stop, start, abrupt stop... He was not phased.

One day as we were reading on our own about the rules of driving, a group of us girls got the giggles. It was another one of those times where we needed to keep those giggles in, and that made the whole situation even funnier.

Well, one of my laughs slipped out, and we were found out. Mr. Warnick was not going to have a group of silly girls misbehaving in his class, and he made sure we knew it. That was one of the only times I saw him get riled up.

The other time was when it was my turn to drive out on the main road. We were driving where the road was hilly and curvy just past Black River. As I was driving up a hill that had a curve at the top, a milk truck came around the bend, and he was in my lane. There was no shoulder in this area. You were either on the road or heading down a ravine. I swerved, and Mr. Warnick said something about not running off the road in a rather excited voice. I told him that truck was in my lane, but I don't think he believed me. There was a little excitement there, but Mr. Warnick settled back into his passenger seat, and we went on our merry way.

"For I am the LORD your God who takes hold of your right hand and says to you, Do not fear; I will help you." Isaiah 41:13

Mr. Warnick managed to get us over our anxieties about driving and got us through our permit test.

The next phase to independent driving would be our parent's job.

Driving Adjustments

With Driver's Ed completed, and permit in hand, I passed my anxieties about driving over to my parents. It was now THEIR car and lives that were at risk as I improved my skills.

Mom was usually in the passenger seat directing me, but I remember a particular day when Dad was with me.

I was driving down Main Street in our boat, I mean car, and I felt like things were going smoothly. As we approached some cars that were parallel parked along the street, Dad started squirming on his side of the seat, and shifting himself as if he was trying to will the car to move to the left. He had more than just white knuckles. He shouted, "Ida Mae, you're about to hit all these cars," as he raised his arms in a bracing panic. He let out a groan in expectation of a collision. What relief when he realized I hadn't hit them! It was a near-miss, according to him. I'm certain his life passed before his eyes.

So, as he was trying to figure out why I couldn't tell that I was so close to those cars, he asked me if I could see where I was in the road. I told him, "Not really."

You see, I stopped growing at the age of twelve, and my height reached a whopping 4'11.5". The car we had for Driver's Ed was smaller than our Plymouth Gran Fury. Seeing out of the school car hadn't been an issue, but trying to see over the steering wheel and hood of our car... Well, you can obviously see there was a problem.

We made it home unharmed, and Dad told Mom all about the incident that nearly happened. They decided I needed some sort of booster seat so that I could see out over the hood of the car. The solution they came up with was to use an old pillow to boost me, but the pillow wasn't enough. So, they folded it which doubled the amount of boost, and that did the trick.

Problem solved!

(You would not believe how much I was teased for having to sit on a pillow to drive.)

Good vision is vital to navigating. I came very close to doing a lot of damage to a lot of cars.

Spiritually speaking, we also need to see where we're going, or we may cause a lot of harm to ourselves and possibly to others with our influence.

"All the paths of the Lord are steadfast love and faithfulness, for those who keep his covenant and his testimonies."

Psalm 25:10(ESV)

"Enter through the narrow gate. For wide is the gate and broad is the road that leads to destruction, and many enter through it. But small is the gate and narrow the road that leads to life, and only a few find it."

Matthew 7:13-14

Shopping for Ideas

At least once a month, we would plan a Saturday to go out to eat and go to the mall to shop. Mom and I would walk around the stores, and Dad would sit and "people watch."

Mom and I loved to shop the sale racks. It was like treasure hunting. But I liked to shop the new items, too, to see what the coming trends were.

I was learning to sew about this time, and one of the reasons I learned to sew was because I had a hard time finding clothes that fit me. I was/am short in stature, and it was just hard to find things that worked. So, this helped encourage my desire to learn to sew. I also liked being unique and having things that were different from what other girls were wearing.

As we shopped, I would make mental notes about what I saw and liked. I carried a little notepad in my purse, and when we got back to the car, I would make notes and drawings about the styles that were coming out. I would go home and look through sewing patterns and see how I could make them look like the new ideas I was seeing. Mom would help me make the adjustments to make what I wanted.

Mom always encouraged me to be unique in all facets of life; what I wore, how I behaved, etc. God calls us to be "unique" in a way too. We are to stand out from the crowd by how we love and not fit into the world.

Romans 12:1-2 says, "Therefore, I urge you, brothers, in view of God's mercy, to offer your bodies as a living sacrifice, holy and pleasing to God—this is your true and proper worship. Do not conform any longer to the pattern of this world, but be transformed by the renewing of your mind."

I encourage you to stand out for the right reasons.

Looking for a Job

Jobs for teens were few in our small town. There was intense competition when someone learned of an opening somewhere.

I remember my mom coming home one day and telling me about a job opportunity at our local radio station. At her behest, I applied and was called for an interview.

I remember meeting the station manager, and he began the interview by asking me why I wanted to work in radio. My ill, unprepared answer was, "I don't know." He went on to have me try out by reading a news script to see how well I would perform. I stumbled and bumbled through that. I was already nervous, and there were words I was having trouble pronouncing. It was a bad interview. I left feeling defeated.

No, I didn't get the job. But what a missed opportunity! If I had been a bit more mature and a bit better prepared, that job could have been a "door-opener" for future employment.

It's one of those moments I look back upon and wonder, "What if...?"

Thankfully an interview isn't required to see if we will fit God's purpose. He wants ALL of us on His team. He accepts the immature and ignorant. He doesn't care about stumbles and bumbles. He offers to equip us with what we need to get His job done. Our part is to be willing to be the worker who doesn't make excuses. We're to be the one who trusts the Leader blindly. No, works won't save us. But through our efforts and our willingness to be used, we show how much we love and trust Him.

"Therefore, my brothers, stand firm. Let nothing move you. Always give yourselves fully to the work of the Lord, because you know that your labor in the Lord is not in vain." 1 Corinthians 15:58

God opens doors of opportunities every day. Just as employers need employees to help get the job accomplished, God needs us to be His helpers. It's not about Him choosing us, but us choosing Him.

A Night of Victory

It was my senior year of high school. My dad had been having issues with his legs feeling numb. A knot had developed on his back around his spine. Tests were run, and cancer was found. Dad was diagnosed with bone cancer. The cancer was attached to one of the vertebrae between his spine and spinal cord.

Dad went through extensive surgery to remove the cancer. The doctors gave him six months to live and told him that he might not regain the use of his legs.

Well, my senior year was in full swing, and I was pretty self-absorbed. I let Dad and Mom deal with all of that while I went on living my life.

One of the big events held in late winter every year at school was the Miss Mustang Pageant. I had been nominated to represent the Thespian Troop.

My dad's surgery had happened around 4 or 5 weeks before this event, and while he was able to use his legs, he was wobbly and on crutches. The surgery had taken a lot out of him, and he was still weak, but he was determined to attend.

It didn't snow often where we lived, but the week of the pageant, it snowed...a lot. We missed that whole week of school, but Mrs. Green said the show must go on because there was no other time to reschedule it.

My mom almost insisted that Dad stay home because if he slipped on the ice, he could destroy all the work the doctors had done to fix his spine, but he was determined to be there.

That night my dad saw me sing a solo, model a dress I had made, and he saw me win first-runner-up.

Years later, I came across some pictures from that night, and there was one of me standing next to my dad on crutches. He had a huge smile on his face.

That night was a victory night for him. Just weeks before, he had been told he might never walk again, and he might not have long to live. But that night, he was living and enjoying the moments he could.

Moments like these are a small taste of the victory we will have when we reach our promised eternal home.

"Thanks be to God! He gives us the victory through our Lord Jesus Christ."

1 Corinthians 15:57

Dad lived ten more years, and he touched many lives in our small town. He spoiled several of the older widows in our congregation by taking them out for ice cream on a nearly weekly basis. There are many ways we can be used to bless others no matter what our health issues may be.

High School Graduation

Graduation was finally here. My family was there to watch me go through the ceremony and help me celebrate.

My sister and I were chatting and I was telling her about the awards I was hoping to receive. I felt I was in good standing for several. I'd done well with my grades that year, and I had been involved in a lot of activities. I was hoping my efforts would be recognized.

Graduation is one of those life markers like no other. All 60 of my classmates and I arrived to receive our diplomas and celebrate this milestone we'd been pushing toward practically our whole lives. One of our teachers had done some research and found that out of the 60 of us, 30 of us had been at that same school the whole time. Half of us had gone through our entire school career together. I thought that was pretty amazing!

It was time for the ceremony to begin. Prayers were given. Speeches were given. Diplomas were given. And awards were given.

Before each award, the teachers would give a little summation about how they came to determine who would receive their particular award. As the awards were handed out, I was not receiving the ones I had hoped to get. I looked over at my sister in the crowd with an "oh well" look since I didn't get any.

There was one final award to be given, and I listened to the teacher list all the qualifications behind their decision for rewarding this person with this particular award. I was going down a list of classmates that I thought would get it. Most of them had already received an award for their outstanding abilities in certain areas. I didn't know which one of them would get this particular award. It could go to any of them from the descriptions they were giving. And so, the anticipation hung in the air as the teacher said, "We give this award to… Ida Mae Walton."

What? Did they just say my name? Wait, they said all that nice stuff about me?? Oh, I was so shocked but so honored. My teachers had given me the award for Best All-Around.

What an absolute honor!

When we got back home after graduation, my sister gave me a hug and said, "You may not have gotten the awards you were hoping for, but you got the best one."

Awards are validation; a recognition of achievement. In 2 Timothy 4:8, there is mention of a reward we have to look forward to:

"Now there is in store for me the crown of righteousness, which the Lord, the righteous Judge, will award to me on that day—and not only to me, but also to all who have longed for His appearing."

God will reward us for how we live our lives. The best one is yet to come.

Acknowledgements

I believe all inspirations comes from God and
I give Him complete credit for this book and
my previous book. He has given me
everything I needed, when I needed it, to put
these books together. Seeing how He did this
has increased my faith and confidence in
Him.

I want to thank my family, Todd, Logan,
and Aubry, for their continued
encouragement and cheerleading for me to do
this second book.

I also want to thank many other family
members, friends and acquaintances who
asked for more. You have enriched my life in
so many ways. Thank you.

About the Cover Artwork

My dad retired early due to health issues, so he was home much of the time.

One day he looked outside and saw a gathering of people at one corner of our field. He went to investigate, and found a group of art students from Williams Baptist College. Their teacher had brought them out to paint our farm! Dad was touched and was able to buy one of the paintings.

When I saw the painting, I fell in love with it and commissioned the artist to paint one for me as well.

These are special treasures to me, and I'm so thankful I'm able to share them with you.

About the Artist

Richard Lee Phillips is a Christian artist who currently resided in Tuckerman, Arkansas where he has been teaching art to high school students for 24 years. He is a graduate of Williams Baptist College near Walnut Ridge, Arkansas and received his master's degree from Arkansas State University in Jonesboro, Arkansas.

In addition to art, Richard enjoys hunting and fishing, and serving at his local church where he leads singing.

Richard believes his family is his best accomplishment of all. He has been married to his wife, Nancy, for 34 years, and they have two children, Colton and Bri. He has four grandchildren that call him Pops, and they bring him much joy.

About the Author

Ida Mae grew up in a small town in rural Arkansas. She was taught the importance of faith in God and her Christian faith grew from there. She now resides in Middle Tennessee with her family, Todd, Logan, and Aubry. She helps teach Bible classes, spends time sewing, and teaching others about sewing and crafting with fabric.

To contact Ida Mae, you may email her at: LobryPublishing@gmail.com

To see photos from Ida Mae's childhood visit:
Instagram
@lobrypublishing

Made in the USA
Monee, IL
08 November 2021